CU00793172

GIRLS GUIDE TO
Basic Beading

DOROTHY WOOD

NEW
HOLLAND

First published in 2015 by New Holland Publishers Pty Ltd
London • Sydney • Auckland

The Chandlery Unit 009 50 Westminster Bridge Road London SE1 7QY United Kingdom
1/66 Gibbes Street Chatswood NSW 2067 Australia
218 Lake Road Northcote Auckland New Zealand

www.newhollandpublishers.com

Copyright © 2015 New Holland Publishers Pty Ltd
Copyright © 2015 in text: Dorothy Wood
Copyright © 2015 in images: Ally Stuart

All rights reserved. No part of this publication may be reproduced, stored in a
retrieval system or transmitted, in any form or by any means, electronic, mechanical,
photocopying, recording or otherwise, without the prior written permission of the
publishers and copyright holders.

A record of this book is held at the British Library and the National Library of Australia.

ISBN 9781742575759

Managing Director: Fiona Schultz
Publisher:Diane Ward
Editor: Simona Hill
Designer: Andrew Quinlan
Photographs: Ally Stuart
Production Director: Olga Dementiev
Printer: Toppan Leefung Printing Ltd

10 9 8 7 6 5 4 3 2 1

Keep up with New Holland Publishers on Facebook
www.facebook.com/NewHollandPublishers

Contents

Introduction

Beading is one of the most enjoyable crafts and it is easy to get started. Most techniques involved are very straightforward. In this book there are techniques and fabulous projects and accessories to make that a complete novice will be able to create in next to no time. If you are a beginner, start with something really simple such as the elasticated bracelet or a basic pair of earrings that don't require special tools. If you work through the techniques section you will learn plenty of new beading skills and before long you'll be able to make a whole range of more challenging projects.

All the basic jewellery techniques, from opening jump rings to making wrapped loops are covered in the techniques section. You will also learn how to work macramé, a simple knotted braid that has become very popular recently. It is one of my favourite techniques and has been used here in innovative ways to make some fabulous pieces of jewellery.

This book has been planned carefully so that the emphasis is on the variety of different styles of jewellery that you can make and how to achieve a particular look. It is easy to buy the exact seed beads shown as many shops have a good stock from the same manufacturer: projects that use larger beads can be harder to copy exactly as shops change their ranges from time to time depending on the season and current trends. When you are ready to make a particular project, take note of the size, shape and type of bead used in the design and then enjoy choosing beads to make your design quite unique.

Even if you don't have a beads shop near by, with the growth of online retailing it is easier than ever to buy beads and all the bits and bobs that you need.

Single-Strand Beaded Necklace

Classic pearls were the inspiration for this pretty necklace. Two sizes of beads create a graduated style and antique gold spacer beads replace the traditional knots to make this quick and easy necklace. You can wear the necklace as a classic string or add an on-trend chain tassel with tiny bead dangles to finish.

YOU WILL NEED

60 cm (24 in) of 0.38 mm (0.015 in)
   19-strand bright, bead stringing wire
5 Miracle beads, lime, 3 mm
20 Miracle beads, lime, 6 mm
10 Miracle beads, lime, 12 mm
55 spacer beads, antique gold, 3 x 1 mm
2 calottes, antique gold, 4 mm
2 size 2 crimp beads
3 jump rings, antique gold, 5 mm
1 jump ring, antique gold, 7 mm
1 lobster clasp, antique gold, 9 mm
1 end cap, antique gold, I.D (internal
   diameter) 8 mm
2 m (2¼ yd) fine chain, antique gold
6 headpins, antique gold
Small bead spring (optional)
Epoxy resin adhesive
Jewellery tools

1 Attach a small bead spring to one end of the bead stringing wire to prevent the beads falling off. Pick up a spacer bead followed by a 6 mm bead then repeat to add 10 of each.

Tip: If you don't have bead springs, a piece of sticky tape folded over the end will stop the beads falling off.

2 Continue adding five 12 mm Miracle beads with spacer beads in between. Add a 5 mm jump ring before the next 12 mm miracle bead and then string the same beads in reverse to add all the beads.

3 Pick up a calotte and a crimp bead on the bead stringing wire (see Techniques, page 99). Secure the crimp with flat-nose pliers. Check the crimp is secure and then trim the wire close to the crimp. Close the calotte with pliers.

4 Hold the necklace up so that the beads all drop down to the calotte and then remove the bead spring. Repeat step 3 to add a calotte to the other end. Attach a 5 mm jump ring to each calotte (see Techniques, page 101). Attach a lobster clasp to one jump ring and a larger jump ring to the other end.

6 Trim the tails and bend the twisted section inside the bundle. Check that the chain tassel will fit into the end cap.

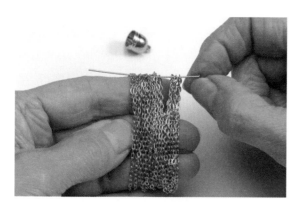

5 To make the tassel, wind the chain around three fingers to make a bundle. With the two tails at the bottom, feed a headpin through one link in each chain at the top. Bend the headpin around and twist the ends together.

7 Mix a little epoxy resin adhesive and apply a small amount inside the end cap at the base and a little more inside around the rim of the end cap. Push the tied end of the chain inside the end cap and leave to dry.

8 Clip the ends of the chains level. You can leave the tassel plain or add some tiny bead dangles. To add bead dangles, pick up a spacer bead and a 4 mm miracle bead on each of five headpins. Make each headpin into a plain loop (see Techniques, page 105). Trim five lengths of the chain shorter and attach a dangle to each. Open the jump ring at the centre of the necklace and attach the chain tassel.

Double-Strand Bead Necklace

Simple knotted necklaces have been a staple of summer jewellery for many years and the trend looks set to continue. This style of necklace is easy to wear and just as easy to make. For an even colour spread down the necklace, attach coloured beads to each knot on one of the strands and only silver heart beads down the other. Add heart charms and dangles at the bottom to bring the design together.

YOU WILL NEED

1.8 m (2 yd) of 1 mm waxed cord, grey
10 metal heart pendant charms, silver-plated, 7 mm
6 metal heart beads, silver-plated, 6 mm
1 metal flower charm, antiqued silver, 10 mm
12 glass beads, multi-coloured, 3 mm
9 seed beads, size 11 (2 mm), to match glass beads
2 ceramic beads, in bright colours, 6 mm
2 flower shape bead caps, gunmetal, 6 mm
12 ball end headpins, gunmetal
5 jump rings, silver-plated, 5 mm
2 crimp ends, silver-plated
Fastening, bolt ring or lobster claw, silver-plated,
1 split ring, silver-plated, 7 mm
Clear nail polish
Jewellery tools

1 Cut 1 m (39 in) of the waxed cord to leave a shorter second piece. Snip the shorter length of cord at an angle at both ends then dip into nail varnish. Smooth the nail varnish between thumb and finger and leave to dry.

2 To make the small bead dangles, pick up a seed bead on a headpin and then a matching 3 mm glass bead. Bend the headpin over at a right angle above the beads and trim to 7 mm. Use round-nose pliers to create a loop (see Techniques, page 105). Make another nine small bead dangles in a variety of shades.

3 To make the larger dangles, pick up a 3 mm glass bead on a headpin, then a matching 6 mm bead and a flower-shape bead cap. Pick up different coloured bead on a second headpin. Following the Techniques on page 105, make two large bead dangles.

4 Open a jump ring (see Techniques, page 103) then pick up a large bead

dangle, a small bead dangle and a heart pendant charm. Close the jump ring. Thread the shorter length of cord through the jump ring and drop to the middle of the cord and tie an overhand knot.

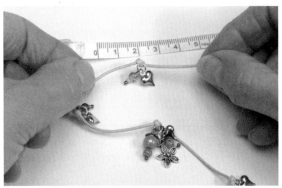

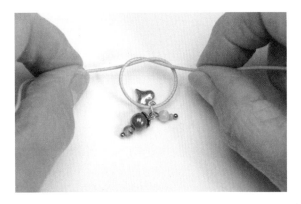

5 Tie another overhand knot on one side leaving a 3 cm (1¼ in) gap. Pick up a metal heart bead threading the cord into the pointed end first then tie another overhand knot to hold the bead securely. Repeat to add another heart bead on the other side of the bead dangles. Leave a 4 cm (1⅝ in) gap before adding another two metal heart beads on each side.

6 Pick up a large bead dangle and a heart pendant charm on a jump ring. Thread onto the remaining piece of cord and tie in the middle with an overhand knot. On a second jump ring, pick up a small bead dangle and a metal flower charm, then attach to the first jump ring.

7 Leave a 4 cm (1⅝ in) gap on both sides and tie an overhand knot. Pick up a small bead dangle and a metal heart pendant charm onto a jump ring. Feed into a single cord of the overhand knot and pull the cord ends to firm up. Repeat on the other side then add three more bead dangles and heart pendant charms leaving the same gap between the knots.

8 Arrange the heart bead length inside the longer length so that the small bead dangles lie between the heart beads for a staggered look. Trim the cord ends level. Attach crimp ends over both cords at each end (see Techniques, page 98). Add a jump ring to each end, then attach the bolt ring fastening to the right hand side and a tab or split ring to the other side.

Tip: You can add an extension chain to the left-hand side jump ring to make the necklace adjustable.

Three-Strand Beaded Necklace

Many bead shops have trays of individual beads arranged in colourways and so it is quite easy to select an eclectic mix of beads. This particular style of necklace has three graduated lengths of beads that are strung from a special finding that reduces the number of strands from three to one. Bring all the elements together with a single metallic colour.

YOU WILL NEED

1.2 m (46 in) of 0.38 mm (0.015 in)
  19-strand bright, bead stringing wire
Mixed selection of beads:
  Round beads, 8 @ 12 mm, 10 @ 10 mm,
    12 @ 8 mm, 5 @ 6 mm
  15 oval fire-polished beads, 6 x 5 mm
  Shell beads, 4 @ 12 mm
  Metal beads, antique silver, 30 @ 4 mm
    round, 11 @ 8 x 2 mm washers
  Seed beads, 18 @ size 8 (3 mm)
2 silver-plated 3-to-1 strand connectors
6 size 2 crimp tubes, silver-plated
6 crimp covers, silver-plated
6 wire guardians, silver-plated
20 cm (8 in) chain, silver-plated, 3 mm
  round links
4 jump rings, silver-plated, 4 mm
1 split ring, silver-plated, 6 mm
Lobster claw fastening, silver-plated
2 bead stopper springs
Jewellery tools
Crimp pliers

1 Arrange the coloured beads, spaced out slightly, in three rows, with smaller beads at each end. Try to create a balanced effect with the same bead in different places in adjacent rows.

2 Once you are happy with the arrangement add some washer beads, three in the top row, four in the next and five in the bottom row. Add small metal beads in between. Check the strand lengths are approximately 17.5, 21.5 and 25.5 cm (7, 8½ in and 10 in).

3 Cut three lengths of bead stringing wire, 35, 40 and 45 cm (14, 16 and 18 in). On each length of wire, pick up three seed beads. Add the beads in the order in which you set them out and finish with three seed beads. Attach the wires into a bead stopper spring and then check the drape of the beads. Adjust the lengths, if required.

Tip: Use bead spring stoppers or a piece of tape to stop the beads falling off the bead stringing wire.

4 Add a crimp tube, then a wire guardian to the first wire. Hook the wire guardian over the 3-to-1 connector, and then feed the tail of the wire back through the crimp tube. Secure the crimp with crimp pliers (see Techniques, page 99–100).

5 Repeat with the first end of the other two beaded wires. Trim the tails to 1.5 cm (5/8 in), then slide the first few beads over the tails to hide. Hold the

short bead string up by the other tail so that the beads all butt together.

6 Pick up a crimp tube and wire guardian. Hook the wire guardian over the other 3-to-1 connector on an outside loop and then feed the tail back through the crimp and a few beads.

7 Make sure the wire is taut, but not overly tight, before securing the crimp again with crimp pliers. Slot the crimp cover over the crimp tube and then close carefully with crimp pliers.

Tip: You can close crimp covers with regular pliers but they may be pushed out of shape.

8 Attach a 10 cm (4 in) length of chain to each 3-to-1 connector using a jump ring (see Techniques, page 103). Attach a lobster claw clasp to one end of the chain and a split ring to the other end using jump rings again.

Long Beaded Charm Necklace

Layered necklaces, in which you hang several bead chains around your neck, is a young, casual style. This necklace made from chain, beads and charms has the same effect, it is just that a shorter beaded chain has been attached to the main chain to create the layer. You can add more than one shorter length if you prefer.

YOU WILL NEED

90 cm (1 yd) chain, antique gold, 4 x 5 mm (approx ¼ in oval) unsoldered links

Charms: 3 hearts, lock and key, coin, antique gold

2 washer-style focal beads, white, 3 mm x 2 cm

6 rose beads, white, 8 mm

6 heart beads, gold, 8 x 10 mm

5 round beads, gold, 7 mm

4 oval beads, gold, 8 x 16 mm

Jump rings, gold-plated, 6 @ 4 mm, 3 @ 7 mm

22 headpins, gold-plated, hard wire

60 cm (24 in) wire, gold-plated, 0.6 mm (22 awg)

Lobster clasp, antique gold

Jewellery tools

1 Make all the beads into plain loop bead links using headpins instead of wire (see Techniques, page 106 step 2). The headpins are made from a harder wire than craft wire and so will hold the loop shape securely. Trim the flat end from each headpin before you start.

2 Join the bead links together randomly in three groups of three, one group of four and one group of eight. Open the chain links to divide the chain into four lengths each 13 cm (5 in). Make another piece 9 cm (3½ in) long, one 18 cm (7 in) long and then three 3-link sections. Set out ready to use later.

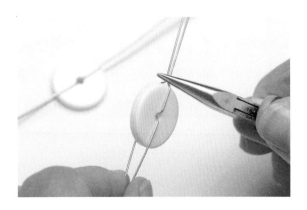

3 Cut the craft wire into four equal pieces. Insert one wire through the hole in the washer-style bead in one direction and a second piece through in the opposite direction so that the bead is centred. Pinch the wires together at each side of the bead.

Tip: Stretch each piece of wire by holding the ends in flat or use snipe-nose pliers and pull the pliers apart.

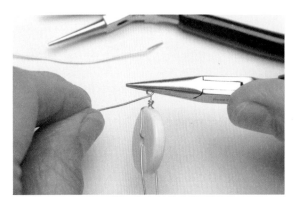

4 Wrap one tail around the other wire twice and trim neatly. Bend the other wire 1 mm ($^1/_{32}$ in) above the wrapping and then use round-nose pliers to make a loop and wrap the wire around twice to complete the wrapped loop

(see Techniques, page 107). The wrapped wire should look like one continuous wrapping.

5 Repeat the wrapping and wrapped loop at the other end of the washer-style bead. Secure the wire on the second washer-style bead in the same way. Open the end link in the 3-link pieces of chain. Attach one piece to each end of one washer bead and one piece to the other washer bead.

6 Opening the end loops, join a 4-bead link length to each short piece of chain on the first washer. Add the 18 cm (7 in) piece of chain to one end, then open the end chain link and attach to the wrapped loop on the second washer bead. Attach the 8-bead link length to the short length of chain on the other end.

8 Using jump rings (see Techniques, page 103) attach the coin bead to the bottom of the main necklace in the centre of the chain and attach a solid heart charm in the centre of the inner necklace chain. Attach two more charms to each side. Finish by attaching the lobster clasp to one end on the necklace and a large jump ring to the other.

7 Attach a 13 cm (5 in) length of chain using a large jump ring to each end of this finished bead chain to create the main necklace length. Join a 13 cm (5 in) length of chain into each large jump ring on the inside of the main necklace. Attach a 3-bead link section to each piece of chain and then join together with the 9 cm (3½ in) piece of chain.

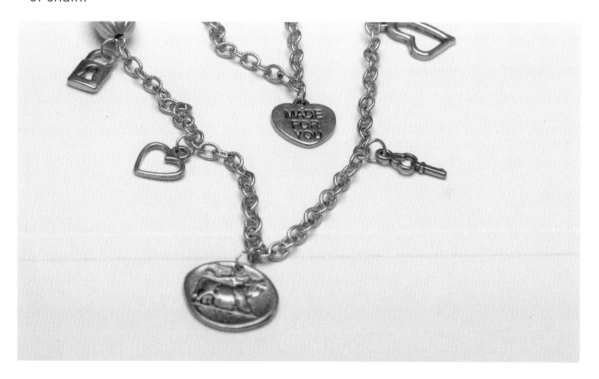

Macramé Necklace

Macramé is often associated with hemp or rustic cords but it can look quite different when worked in a silky rattail cord. The cord creates a soft braid that holds its shape well, curving around to create the base of this short necklace. Decorate the braid with beautiful Swarovski Elements Fancy Stones in different shapes, each in its own specially shaped setting.

YOU WILL NEED

Swarovski Elements:
- 1 oval Fancy Stone 4120, amethyst, 18 x 13 mm
- 2 square Fancy Stones 4470, crystal blue, 12 mm
- 2 navette Fancy Stones 4228, black diamond, 15 mm
- 2 drop Fancy Stones 4328, Montana, 10 x 6 mm

Settings, two-hole, silver-plated, to fit the Fancy Stones

50 cm (20 in) of 0.4 mm (26 awg) craft wire, silver-plated

2 ribbon crimp ends, silver-plated, 10 mm

Necklace fastening

5.25m (5¾ yd) of 2 mm rattail, silver blue

Beading thread and needle

Jewellery tools

1 Cut a 1.25 m (1³/₈ yd) length of rattail and fold in half to make the 'core' cords. Secure each pair of ends to the macramé board. Tie the remaining length of rattail around the two core cords with an overhand knot and flip the knot to the reverse side.

2 Following the technique on page 96–97, work the square knot macramé till the core cords are covered with knots. Tape each end to secure it temporarily. Sew across with tiny running stitches after the last knot at one end to secure the cords. Sew in the thread ends.

3 Trim the cords to 3 mm (1/8 in) and then tuck inside the ribbon crimp end. Use nylon jaw pliers to secure the ribbon crimp end over the raw ends. Check the length of the necklace and stitch the other end at the correct length, before trimming and fitting the ribbon crimp end (see page 98).

Tip: 46 cm (18 in) is an average length for a short necklace, but adjust as necessary to suit yourself.

4 Set the Fancy Stones into their individual settings: place the stone level in the appropriate setting and then use snipe-nose pliers to flatten the metal lugs one at a time onto the stone.

5 Feed a length of wire through from the centre of the oval stone setting and out of one of the 'top' holes. Feed the wire through two holes in the square fancy stone, then the Navette and finally the two holes at the pointy end of the drop Fancy Stone.

6 Work back through the lower holes in the Fancy Stones and then add the same beads on the other side of the oval, going through the lower holes first this time. Take the wire back through the top holes and out in the middle of the centre oval setting.

7 Pull the wires taut so that the stones all butt together and in a slightly curved shape. Twist the wires together, trim and tuck inside the setting.

8 Arrange the stones in the centre of the macramé braid. Stitch it onto the braid using a beading thread. Sew in the ends securely. Attach a necklace fastening to the ribbon crimp ends. Depending on the style you may need to use jump rings to attach (see Techniques, page 103).

Beaded Ribbon Necklace

This simple necklace is made from large hole beads that are simply strung onto ribbon. It has no fastening as the ribbon is tied in a bow at the back of the neck. It isn't likely that you will be able to find exactly these beads but similar large hole beads will give the same effect. These pretty floral drop beads are opaque plastic but you could also use translucent Lucite beads.

YOU WILL NEED

7 fabric-covered beads, 2 cm round
6 ceramic beads, 16 x 12 mm
14 clay beads, matte mixed pastels,
  8 mm round
6 ceramic wedge beads, matte cream and
  terracotta, 5 x 14 mm
4 metal washer beads, silver-plated,
  9 x 16 mm
18 flower drop beads, mixed pastels,
  5 x 10 mm
36 pearls, ivory, 3 mm round
5 seed beads, dark cream, size 8 (3 mm)
18 headpins, silver-plated
2 headpins, silver-plated, 7 cm (2¾ in) long
1.5 m of 2 cm (60 in of ¾ in) wide organza
  ribbon, dark cream
Large tapestry needle
5 jump rings, silver-plated, 7 mm
Jewellery tools

1 Set one large ceramic bead, one fabric-covered bead and a matte clay bead aside. String the other beads onto the ribbon in a random order to make a row of beads about 35 cm (14 in) long. Arrange in the middle of the ribbon.

2 Put one of the flower drop beads to one side and then create bead dangles with the rest: pick up a pearl, flower bead, and a pearl on a regular headpin. Bend the headpin over after the beads, trim to 7 mm ($^9/_{32}$ in). Make a loop with round-nose pliers (see Technique, page 105). Repeat with the remaining flower beads.

Tip: As it is a tight fit, use snipe-nose pliers to add the small flower bead dangles to the necklace.

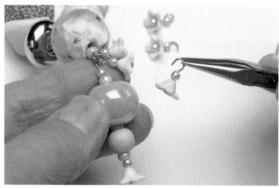

3 On a long headpin, pick up a pearl, flower bead, pearl, seed bead, matte ceramic bead, seed bead, large ceramic bead, a seed bead and a pearl. Make a bead dangle (see Techniques, page 105). Trim the flat end from the other long headpin. Make a bead link with a seed bead, fabric-covered bead and a seed bead. (see Techniques, page 106).

4 Attach a bead link to the long-head pin dangle. Open a jump ring and attach the large bead dangle just made. Separate two beads in the middle of the necklace and hook the jump ring over the ribbon. Close the jump ring again (see Techniques, page 103).

5 Open a jump ring again and pick up two different colours of flower bead dangle. Repeat to make three more beaded jump rings. Add a jump ring between the beads, two on one side of the centre dangle and two on the other, not necessarily at the same height.

6 Add the remaining flower bead links onto the two loops in the centre of the long bead dangle, adding one at a time to create a cluster effect. Tie an overhand knot with each end of ribbon and manoeuvre it down next to the beads to secure. Tie the ribbon in a bow at the back of the neck.

Wrap Friendship Bracelet

Wrap bracelets are made using a method of braiding in which thread loops each side of a thicker cord, and then doubles back on itself to create the 'switchback' technique. Use a single row of beads to create a long thin bracelet that wraps around your wrist several times or try three bead rows for a wider style.

YOU WILL NEED

1 m (1 yd) of 1 mm leather cord, turquoise
2 m (2¼ yd) Superlon™ thread, lime
Miracle beads, 3 mm, 35 orange,
   35 turquoise
30 washer beads, gold, 1.5 x 5 mm
Small metal button
Macramé board or cork pin board
Darning needle
Small scissors
Map pins

1 Thread the cord up through one hole in the button and drop it down to the middle of the cord. Thread the end back down through the other hole. Loop a short length of cord around the button and tuck into the slots at the top of the board. Push the ends into a slot at the base of the board.

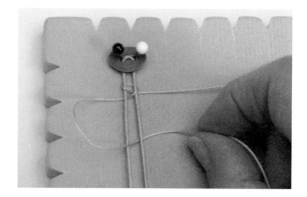

2 Feed the Superlon thread under both leather cords and pull through until both thread ends are the same length. Work a section of switchback braid to create a shank under the button: to start, take the left thread over the left cord and under the right-hand cord so that both threads are out to the right.

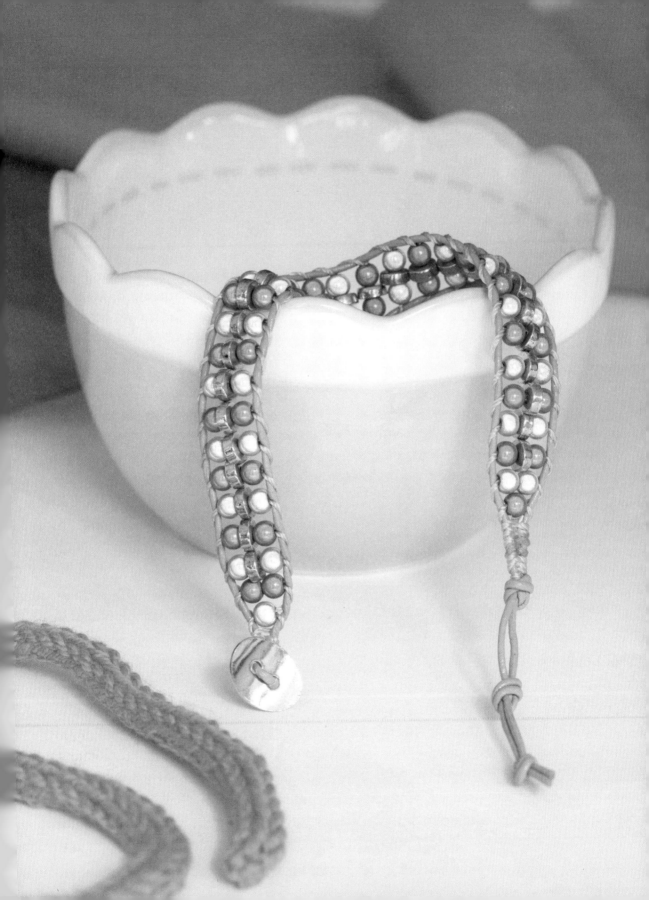

3 *Take the top right thread over the right cord and under the left cord. Switchback with the same cord over the left and under the right. Repeat from * five or six times to create the shank, finishing with both threads sticking out on opposite sides under the leather cord.

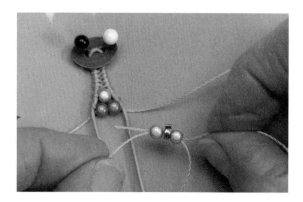

4 Pick up a 3 mm turquoise bead on the left thread and feed the right thread through the bead in the opposite direction. Pull the threads through so that the bead is sitting between the leather cords. Tuck the cords under the leather cord at each side.

Tip: Dip both ends of the Superlon in clear nail varnish and leave to dry to create an 'in built' needle before you start.

5 Repeat step 4 but pick up two orange beads, 3 mm, on the left thread. To start the main section of the bracelet, pick up a turquoise bead, a washer bead and another turquoise bead. Feed the right thread through all three beads in the opposite direction. Pull the threads taut and tuck under the leather cord at each side.

6 Continue adding the two round beads with a washer between them in the same way, alternating between orange and turquoise beads until the section with three beads in each row measures 13 cm (5 in). Reduce the beads in the next two rows to match the other end.

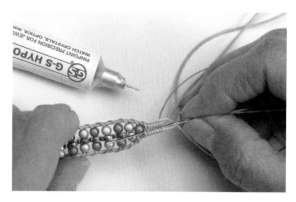

7 Work a short section of switchback technique just with the cords. Sew the ends through the switchback section then add a drop of superglue or beading glue to secure before trimming.

8 Tie the two ends of leather in an overhand knot so that the knot is next to the switchback section. Tie another overhand knot leaving a gap just large enough to thread the button through. Repeat again to make a second buttonhole slot, if required, to make the bracelet adjustable. Trim the ends near the knot.

Macramé Bracelet with Rhinestones

Macramé is such a versatile technique – it looks great when simply knotted but is transformed with the addition of beads. Usually beads are added on the outer cords before you tie the next knot but this design incorporates cup chain or rhinestones too for a bit of sparkle. Finish the bracelet with a simple slider fastening.

● ●

YOU WILL NEED

80 cm (32 in) of 1 mm round leather cord, pink metallic

2.5m (2¹/₈ yd) Superlon™ thread, dusty pink

Cup chain, silver-plated, eighteen 4 mm set stones

36 fire polished round beads, silver, 4 mm

Macramé board

Superglue or jewellery glue

Small scissors

1 Cut the leather into two equal pieces and secure into slots at the each end of the macramé board. If you don't have a macramé board, tape to the work surface at each end.

2 Pass a 1.5 m (60 in) length of Superlon thread under both leather cords and tie in an overhand knot (see Techniques, page 94), then flip the knot to the underside so that there is just a single bar on the front of the leather cords.

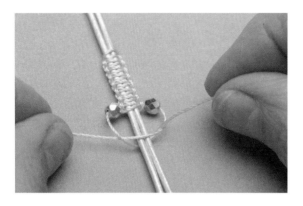

3 Following the instructions for square knot on page 96–97, work 2 cm (¾ in) of braid. Before you tie the next knot pick up a 4 mm round bead on each end of the Superlon threads and drop the beads down to the work. Work the first half of the square knot but don't pull taut.

4 Tuck the cup chain under the right-hand cord that is looping over the leather cord and then pull the knot taut. Work the second half of the square knot so that the threads lie between the first and second rhinestones in the cup chain.

Tip: If you can't work out which thread to start with, remember you always pass the thread that is sticking up from the knot under the leather cords next.

5 Continue picking up a 4 mm round bead on each thread before tying a square knot between the rhinestones. Once you have reached the end of the cup chain, work a 2 cm (¾ in) length of plain macramé at the end to match the beginning.

6 Add a drop of superglue where the tails emerge from the macramé and then sew the ends back through the square knots and trim the ends.

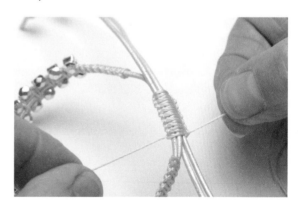

7 Form the bracelet into a circle so that the pairs of leather cord ends are overlapping and facing in opposite directions. Tie a 1 m (1 yd) length of Superlon thread around all four

leather cords. Flip the knot to the inside of the bracelet and then work a 2 cm (¾ in) length of macramé to create a slider mechanism.

8 Oversew back down the edge of the macramé slider mechanism all the way along, with each tail, and then add a drop of glue and leave to dry before trimming the ends of the thread. Tie double overhand knots on each of the leather tails and trim.

Elastic Beaded Bracelet

Beads strung onto elastic cord make up into the simplest bracelet, but that doesn't mean it has to be ordinary. You can choose a selection of different coloured beads or keep to the same colour and make a complementary bracelet so that you can wear two or even three together. Adding spacers, metal beads or charms makes a simple bracelet a little special.

· ·

YOU WILL NEED
For both bracelets:
1 m (1 yd) of 0.5 mm elastic cord
Round cat's eye glass beads, 7 mm,
    20 blue, 23 yellow
6 metal beads, silver-plated, 6 mm
31 square wire rings, silver-plated, 6 mm
Superglue or jewellery glue
Charms: heart 1.5 cm, solid metal ring
    1.5 cm
Seed bead, size 11 (2 mm)
Headpin, silver-plated
2 jump rings, silver-plated, 5 mm
Small scissors

1 Cut a 50 cm (20 in) length of elastic cord and pull the ends apart to take out some of the stretch. Pick up 18 glass beads and drop to the middle of the elastic.

Tip: Stretching the elastic before you start ensures that the bracelets will not become loose over time.

2 Pick up a square wire ring, a round glass bead and another square wire ring on each end. Pick up five metal beads and four square wire rings alternately on one end of the elastic cord.

3 Feed one end of the elastic cord all the way through the beads again to come back out at the same point as the other tail. Pull the ends of the elastic cord until you take up all the slack but not so tight that the bracelet is distorted.

4 Tie a surgeon's knot in the elastic cord. This is like a reef knot but with an extra wrap (see Techniques, page 95). Take the left cord over the right and under. Then take the right cord over the left twice. Pull the elastic cord ends to firm the knot.

Variation: String alternate square wire rings and round glass beads onto the elastic cord and tie off as before. Add a heart charm with a jump ring to one square wire ring. Use a second jump ring to attach a large metal ring and bead dangle to the first jump ring.

5 Feed one tail through the adjacent metal bead. Add a drop of superglue or jewellery glue over the knot and then quickly tug the tail to pull the knot inside the bead. Trim the tails and leave to dry for several hours before wearing.

Plaited Leather Bracelet

Beading shops stock all sorts of cords and braids that can be incorporated into jewellery designs. Look out for flat leather or plaited leather in bright colours that can be strung with beads and chain to create a layered bracelet. Alternatively you can plait your own leather cord or use a fine macramé braid instead.

• •

YOU WILL NEED

Approximately 13 round beads, bright
  yellow/pink, 7 mm
12 Rondelle beads, bright yellow, 8 x 4 mm
20 cm (8 in) of 3 mm (1/8 in) wide plaited
  (braided) leather, bright yellow
20 cm (8 in) of 5 x 8 mm links curb chain,
  gold-plated
20 cm (8 in) of 0.38 mm (0.015 in) 19-strand
  bright bead stringing wire
Jump rings, gold-plated, 12 @ 4 mm,
  2 @ 6 mm
2 calottes, gold-plated, 4 mm
2 crimp beads, size 1
2 ribbon crimps, gold-plated, 5 mm wide
Charms, gold-plated, handbag and hand
Lobster claw clasp, gold-plated
Jewellery tools

1 Attach a ribbon crimp to the end of the plaited leather (see Techniques, page 98) then attach a small jump ring. Attach a small jump ring to the end of the chain too (see Techniques, page 103).

2 Pick up a crimp bead on the end of the bead stringing wire and use snipe-nose pliers to flatten near the end. Secure a calotte over the crimp and then attach to a small jump ring (see Techniques, pages 99–101).

Tip: If you are using a clamshell-type of calotte, thread the bead stringing wire through the hole in the hinge before securing the crimp bead.

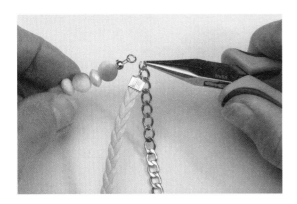

3 Open another small jump ring and pick up the ribbon crimp end on the plaited leather. On one side of the leather, pick up the jump ring on the end of the chain and at the other side the string of beads. Close the jump ring.

4 Attach the lobster clasp to the end jump ring with another small jump ring. Set the bracelet out flat. Measure from the tip of the lobster clasp along the plaited leather and mark where it measures 17.5 cm (6½ in). This is the standard bracelet length but can be adjusted to suit your wrist.

5 Trim the leather and attach a ribbon crimp end and small jump ring. Trim the chain to the same length and add a small jump ring. Add or remove beads to the same length. Attach a crimp bead to the other end of beading wire making sure the beads all butt together. Attach a calotte and then a small jump ring.

6 Add the three strands of the bracelet to another small jump ring and then attach a large jump ring with another small jump ring. Attach a handbag charm and handmade hand individually with small jump rings to a small jump ring at one end of the bracelet.

Cuff Beaded Bracelet

Neon colours have such a wow factor and so this vibrant variegated knotting cord makes a really striking braid as the base of this pretty bracelet. Choose beads that blend in with the braid, adding some softer shades to tone down the bright neon and give the bracelet a classier look.

• •

YOU WILL NEED

2.5 m (2¾ yd) of 1.5 mm Chinese knotting cord, bright variegated

13 round beads, bright pink, 6 mm

13 round facetted beads, soft green, 6 mm

1 string 25 cm (10 in) spacer beads, bright variegated

Superlon™ cord

Small square of felt

Sewing needle and thread

Darning needle

2 ribbon crimps, antique silver, 2 cm (¾ in)

Macramé board

4 bead springs, small

Small scissors

Nylon jaw pliers

1 Cut two lengths of knotting cord each 25 cm (10 in) and secure to the macramé board. Cut two lengths of knotting cord each 1 m (39 in) and secure one on each side of the shorter cords. Work square knot macramé to make a 17 cm (6½ in) length (see Techniques, pages 96–97).

2 String the round beads and facetted beads alternately onto Superlon cord, adding a brightly coloured spacer bead between each bead to make a 16 cm (6¾ in) length.

3 String the same length of washer beads onto Superlon cord. Rearrange or choose particular colours of the washer beads, if necessary, to match the macramé braid.

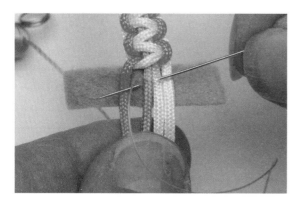 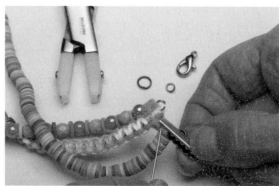

4 Cut 2 strips of felt each 5 x 25 mm (¼ x 1 in). Arrange the macramé in the middle of one strip so that the knots are against the felt. Sew backstitch over the cords to secure to the felt, taking some stitches through the cords. Sew in the ends.

5 Use a darning needle to sew the Superlon cord into the felt. Secure with a couple of back stitches so that the beads will lie against the macramé cord at each side. Fold the felt over at each side and sew the two layers of felt together.

Tip: Cross the strings of beads over the macramé and stitch on the opposite side at the other end.

6 Trim the top edge to remove the thread and cord tails and then secure the ribbon crimp over the top using nylon jaw pliers (see Techniques, page 98). Repeat to secure the braid and strings of beads at the other end. Attach a fastening to the ribbon crimp ends with jump rings (see Techniques, page 103).

Elegant Bracelet

Pearls strung onto knotted silk cord make classic bracelet design. You can buy freshwater pearls in a range of unusual colours and when strung with a matching silk cord look incredibly stylish. Add some pretty charms to make it quite unique. This easy stringing technique, using calottes, is ideal for a beginner.

YOU WILL NEED

Approximately 25 natural pearls, plum,
   5 x 7 mm
Natural silk thread, no 5 (0.65 mm)
2 calottes, silver-plated, 4 mm
4 crimp beads, size 1
2 jump rings, silver-plated, 5 mm
Toggle fastening, silver-plated
2 charms, silver-plated
Darning needle
Small scissors
Jewellery tools

1 Unwind the whole length of silk thread from the bobbin and straighten the integral twisted wire needle. Tie an overhand knot (see Techniques, page 94) about 5 cm (2 in) from the end of the silk thread. Pick up a pearl and drop down to the knot.

2 Tie a loose second overhand knot just below the pearl. Insert the darning needle into the loop of the knot and lift the knot behind the pearl.

3 Hold the needle with the knot behind the pearl. As you pull the silk thread the needle will guide the knot up to the pearl. The secret is to slowly draw out the needle as the knot tightens so that the knot ends up right next to the pearl.

4 Thread on another pearl and push up against the knot as you pull on the silk thread. This will also help to firm up the knot right against the previous pearl. Continue working an overhand knot after each pearl until you have a string of pearls about 16 cm (6¼ in) long.

5 Thread two crimp beads onto the short tail of the pearl string. Squeeze the crimp beads flat one at a time so that they are sitting close to the knot and then trim the thread end (see Techniques, page 99).

Tip: If you are using a clam shell-style of calotte (with the hole in the hinge) you need to thread the calotte on to the thread before the two crimp beads.

6 Tuck both crimps inside the calotte – you may need to fold them over one on top of the other – then close the calotte using snipe-nose pliers. Add a jump ring on the end of the calotte and squeeze flat with snipe-nose pliers (see Techniques, page 101).

7 Attach the T-bar of the toggle fastening to the jump ring. Check the length of the bracelet allowing for adding a calotte and the ring end of the toggle fastening and add another one or two pearls, if required, finishing with an overhand knot.

8 On this end, add another calotte with two crimp beads as before. Attach a jump ring and then the loop end of the fastening. Attach a charm or two to the small jump ring next to the loop end fastening. Depending on the style of charm use a jump ring or thread the charms onto a headpin and make a wrapped loop dangle.

Looped Earrings

Seed beads are a generic term for a range of small beads that come in different colours, finishes and sizes. For this design, size 11 matte beads have been strung with some slightly larger shiny gold seed beads as a detail. If you'd prefer copper or silver, change the plating colour on the findings to match.

YOU WILL NEED

1.2 m (47 in) of 0.38 mm (0.015 in) 19-strand gilt bead stringing wire

Seed beads, size 11 (2 mm), opaque matte lime, frosted yellow and opaque matte plum

24 seed beads, size 8 (3 mm), gold

2 cat's eye round beads, yellow, 7 mm

Bead stringing wire, 19-strand, 0.38 mm (0.015 in) gilt

12 crimp tubes, gold-plated, 1.5 mm (size 2)

Micro crimp pliers

2 jump rings, gold-plated, 6 mm

2 earring wires, gold-plated

Jewellery tools

Small bead springs

1 Cut three lengths of bead stringing wire each 20 cm (8 in). Pick up 19 size 11 lime seed beads on one length, then add 3 gold seed beads, each size 8, with lime in between. Finish with 19 lime seed beads.

Tip: Put a bead spring or piece of tape on one end of the bead stringing wire to stop the beads falling off.

2 Pick up a crimp tube on one end of the wire. Feed the tail back down through the crimp tube and pull through to make a small loop on the wire. Secure the crimp tube with crimp pliers (see Techniques, pages 99–100).

3 Trim the tail to 1 cm (3/8 in) and feed the beads over the tail to hide. Hold by the other tail to let all the seed beads drop down to the crimp tube. Pick up a second crimp tube, tuck the tail back down through the tube and through 6 or 7 seed beads.

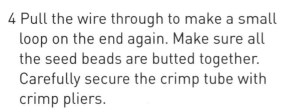

4 Pull the wire through to make a small loop on the end again. Make sure all the seed beads are butted together. Carefully secure the crimp tube with crimp pliers.

Tip: Take care that you don't break a seed bead with the crimp pliers when securing the crimp tube at the other end.

5 Make a second length of seed beads using the yellow seed beads. Pick up 25 size 11, then four of the size 8 gold, alternating with yellow, then another 25 yellow. Secure at each end with crimp tubes as before.

6 Make a third length of seed beads using plum. Pick up 28 size 11, then five of the size 8 gold, alternating with lime, then another 28 plum. Secure at each end with crimp tubes as before.

7 Open a jump ring (see Techniques, page 103) and feed one end of the lime bead string on. Make sure the bead strand isn't twisted and hook the other end onto the jump ring. Add the yellow beads, one loop at each side and then the plum.

8 Check the loops are lying fairly straight and then close the jump ring. Make a bead link using the yellow cat's eye bead and a gold-plated headpin (see Techniques, page 106). Make sure the loops at each end of the bead link are at right angles to one another so that the earrings hang correctly. Attach to the jump ring and then add the earring wire. Make a second earring to match.

Wire-Wrapped Earrings

To make them extra special, these earrings have been made with tiny round semi-precious beads and as a result have small holes that mean you need to use very fine wire and headpins to make the design. The little bird charm is very cute but you can choose a different charm, perhaps tiny cats or hearts, so long as the hole goes through the middle vertically.

YOU WILL NEED

Small round semi-precious beads, 2 mm, approximately 90 plum and 40 lilac
50 cm (20 in) of wire, gold-plated, 0.8 mm (20 awg)
1 m (1 yd) of wire, gold-plated, 0.4 mm (26 awg)
2 headpins, gold-plated, fine (0.4 mm or less)
2 bird charms, gold colour
2 earring wires, gold-plated
Jewellery tools

1 Cut the 0.8 mm (20 awg) wire in half. Hold each end with flat-nose pliers and pull both ends to straighten the wire (you can put one end in a vice too). Hold the wire in the middle with flat or snipe-nose pliers and bend in half to create a 'v' shape.

2 Pull each wire tail through between finger and thumb so that it bends in a gentle curve outward. Try not to kink the wire. Cross the wires over about 5.5 cm (2 1/8 in) from the 'v' shape and use snipe-nose pliers to bend the wires back where they cross so that the two tails are parallel above the petal shape.

3 Hold both straight wires near the tip of the round-nose pliers and bend one wire out at right angles. Use the round-nose pliers to create a wrapped loop around both straight bits of wire at the top of the petal shape. Trim both tails (see Techniques, page 107).

4 Wrap the end of a 40 cm (16 in) length of 0.4 mm (26 awg) wire around both thicker wires under the wrapped loop to secure. Wind around one side of the petal shape a couple of turns and then pick up a small round plum bead. If the wire came over the top of the thicker wire before adding the bead go under the wire at the other side and vice versa. Wrap the wire a couple of times again.

Tip: Alternating the wrapping over the wire at one side and under the wire at the other keeps the beading even.

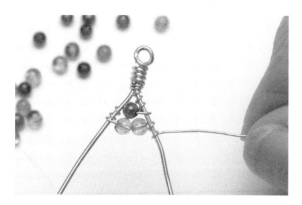

5 Pick up two lilac beads on the wire and take the wire across the petal shape so that the beads are sitting against the first bead. Wind the wire

a couple of times around the thicker wire ready to add the next row of beads.

6 Next row, pick up three lilac beads, then four plum beads, and so on adding one lilac row then two plum rows until you are about half way down the petal shape finishing with an even number of beads. Wrap the wire around once to secure and then wrap back up the petal shape between the next two rows to secure the tail. Trim the fine wire.

7 To make the headpin dangle, pick up a plum and lilac round bead on a fine headpin, then the bird charm and three more round beads. Pre-form a wrapped loop on the end (see Techniques, page 107) and attach to the middle of the last bead row.

8 Complete the wrapping on the dangle and trim neatly. Attach an earring wire to the wrapped loop at the top of the earring. Make a second earring to match.

Dangly Bead Earrings

Earrings can be made in all shapes and sizes and this style, using bead dangles and bead links is one of the most versatile designs. The link between the two sets of beads allows the beads to move about when you are wearing them. You can make longer earrings by adding a second link or attach some individual bead dangles alongside the pearl.

YOU WILL NEED

Swarovski elements:

    4 round crystal beads 5000, tangerine, 3 mm

    2 round crystal pearls 5810, blackberry, 8 mm

    2 round drop crystal pearls 5816, blackberry, 3 mm

    2 drop crystal pearls, blackberry, half drilled, 15 x 8 mm

4 headpins, copper

2 earring wires, copper

GS cement jewellery glue

Jewellery tools

1 Trim the flat head off the four headpins. Make a plain loop on one end of all four headpins to make eyepins (see Techniques, page 106).

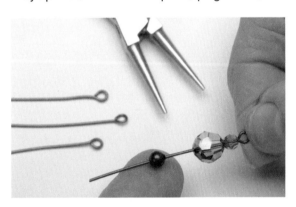

2 Pick up a 3 mm round tangerine bead, an 8 mm round blackberry bead and a 3 mm round blackberry pearl on one of the prepared eyepins.

3 Bend the headpin over at right angles above the pearl and then trim to 7 mm ($^9/_{32}$ in). Form a loop using round-nose pliers (see Techniques, page 105).

4 Push one of the other headpins into the hole in the drop pearl to see how deep the hole is. Pick up a 3 mm tangerine bead on one of the prepared headpins and then trim the headpin to the same length as the depth of the hole.

5 Apply a tiny amount of bead jewellery glue on the end of the headpin and then push it into the hole in the drop pearl. Wipe off any excess and leave to dry for 24 hours.

Tip: If you are using regular drop pearls, pick up the pearl and then the tangerine bead on an untrimmed headpin instead.

6 Open the one of the loops on the bead link and attach the drop pearl dangle. Attach the earring wire to the other end. Make a second earring to match.

Knotted Leather Earrings

Bohemian-style jewellery has a fresh look that is easy to recreate using colourful beads and leather cord. This simple style uses a fine leather cord that is held in place with a homemade spring. Look for a decorative bead, such as this striped cube that picks up the colours in the round beads so that the whole design works as a whole.

. . . .

YOU WILL NEED
40 cm (16 in) of 1 mm leather cord, deep blue
20 cm (8 in) of 0.7 mm (21 awg) wire, gold-plated
2 washer beads, gold, 1 x 5 mm
2 round metal beads, gold, 6 mm
Round ceramic beads, 2 orange and 2 lemon, 6 mm
2 facetted round beads, petrol blue, 6 mm
2 stripe cube beads, 8 mm
Wrapping mandrel
2 earring wires, gold-plated
Jewellery tools

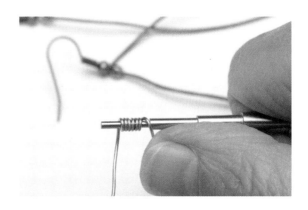

1 Cut the leather cord in half and feed one length through each earring wire. Make a tight spring with a 2–3 mm internal diameter. Wrap the wire around the wrapping mandrel five times to make a tight spring. Trim both ends on the same side. Make a second spring in the same way.

Tip: You can use a fine knitting needle or even a bamboo skewer or cocktail stick to make the spring instead.

2 Feed both tails of leather cord into a spring so that the tails are the same length and the spring is close to the earring wire loop. Turn the spring so that the trimmed ends are at the back and lying between the cords. Use snipe-nose pliers to squeeze the top coil slightly to secure. Repeat with the other earring.

3 Tie an overhand knot (see Techniques, page 94) on one tail of leather cord and manouevre it up to about 1.5 cm (5/8 in) below the spring before pulling taut.

4 Pick up a facetted bead, a washer, an orange ceramic bead, a washer and a pink ceramic bead. Tie an overhand knot under the beads so that they are secured with no gaps between the knots.

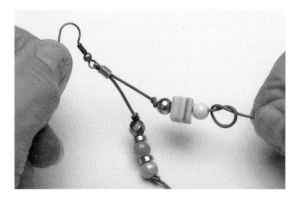

5 Tie an overhand knot at the same height on the second strand of leather. Pick up a round metal bead, a decorative bead and a lemon ceramic bead. Tie another overhand knot.

6 Make another earring to match, adding the beads to the opposite cords on the second earring so that it is a mirror image of the first. Once you are happy with the height and arrangement of beads, trim the leather about 5 mm (¼ in) from the bottom overhand knots on each earring.

Beaded Three-Strand Earrings

Delica beads are cylindrical beads that create a fabulous tubular effect on the earring strands. When making the long bead links it is better to start with a headpin rather than wire as the headpin is harder wire and less likely to bend out of shape. It is easier to make loops the same size at each end if you make both loops yourself, rather than starting with an eyepin.

YOU WILL NEED

Miyuki Delica beads, size 10 (2.2 mm), opaque orange (722), matte opaque orange AB (872), matte opaque red AB (874), opaque turquoise green lustre (217), dura galvanized matte gold (1832F)

6 fire-polished beads, matte metallic Aztec gold, 4 mm

Headpins, gold-plated, six @ 7.5 cm (3 in) and six @ 3.5 cm (1½ in)

2 jump rings, gold-plated, 5 mm

2 earring wires, gold-plated

Jewellery tools

1 Pick up the following delicas on a 7.5 cm (3 in) headpin: 1 x gold, 7 x turquoise, 1 x gold, 8 x orange AB, 1 x gold, 3 x red AB, 1 x gold, 8 x orange, 1 x gold.

Tip: Delica beads are available in different sizes so ensure you choose a size 10 or 11 to get the right effect.

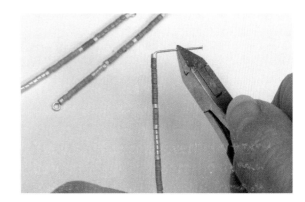

2 Use round-nose pliers to make a small loop at the end of the headpin (see Techniques, page 106). Bend the headpin over at right angles directly above the beads at the other end. Trim the tail (removing the flat end of

the headpin) to 7 mm and then make a loop at this end too.

3 Pick up the following delicas on another 7.5 cm (3 in) headpin:
1 x gold, 8 x orange AB, 1 x gold, 3 x turquoise, 1 x gold, 7 x orange, 1 x gold, 8 x red AB, 1 x gold. Make into a long bead link again as step 2.

4 To make the third long bead link, pick up the following delicas on a 7.5 cm (3 in) headpin: 1 x gold, 10 x red AB, 1 x gold, 3 x orange, 1 x gold, 5 x turquoise, 1 x gold, 8 x orange AB, 1 x gold.

5 On a shorter gold-plated headpin, pick up a turquoise delica, then a 4 mm Aztec gold fire-polished bead. Use the tips of the snipe-nose pliers to hold the headpin 1 mm away from the facetted bead and bend the headpin at right angles. Trim to 7 mm (9/32 in) and form a loop with round-nose pliers.

6 Make another two headpin dangles, one with an orange AB delica and the other with a red AB. Attach the small headpin dangles to the matching colour of bead link.

7 Attach all three long headpin links to an opened jump ring and then attach an earring wire before closing the jump ring again (see Techniques, page 103). Use the tips of snipe-nose pliers to hold the left-hand bead link at the top and bend over slightly inwards.

8 Repeat with the bead link on the other side, bending the loop at the top in the opposite direction so that all three bead links hang straight. Make a second earring to match.

Elegant Earrings

Swarovski crystals and pearls transform a simple design into stunning elegant earrings that would look fabulous worn with a prom dress or going to another special celebration. The crystal stones are already set and so all you need to do is hang some chain and bead dangles to create the earrings. You are working on a small scale but the effort is well worth it!

YOU WILL NEED

Swarovski Elements:

  2 round set stones 4 holes sterling silver 117704, 8 mm (S39), foiled crystal

  2 butterfly beads 5754, aquamarine, 8 mm

  10 round beads 5000, crystal comet argent light, 3 mm

  8 crystal pearls 5810, turquoise, 4 mm

14 ball end headpins, silver-plated

30 cm (12 in) of 2.5 mm (1/8 in) rollo chain, round links, silver-plated

2 earring posts, glue on, silver-plated

Epoxy resin adhesive

Jewellery tools

1 Cut the chain into four pieces measuring 15, 20, 25 and 30 links (approximately 2 cm (¾ in) for the shortest and then 5 mm (¼ in) longer for each subsequent length. Cut another set for the second earring. Arrange one set on the beading mat in order: 15, 20, 30 and 25 links.

2 Pick up a butterfly bead on a ball end headpin and then add a 3 mm round bead. Pre-form a wrapped loop and attach to the longest length of chain before completing the wrapping (see Techniques, page 107). Trim the end flush.

3 Pick up a 4 mm pearl then a 3 mm round bead on a ball end headpin, pre-form a wrapped loop and attach to the shortest length of chain. Repeat to add a bead dangle to the other two lengths of chain.

4 Make another wrapped loop bead dangle and at the pre-formed stage attach to the sixth link from the top of the butterfly chain. Complete the wrapping and trim the end flush.

5 Thread a ball end headpin straight through two opposite holes in the round stone setting. Hold the headpin in the tips of the round-nose pliers and bend the headpin over at right angles. Pre-form a loop and attach the two shorter lengths of prepared chain. Complete the wrapped loop and trim.

6 Repeat step 5 to add the other two chain lengths to the other side of the round stone setting.

7 Make a second earring in a mirror image of the first. Use epoxy resin adhesive to attach an earring post to the back of each round stone setting. Leave to dry for 24 hours before wearing.

Tip: When you are adding the chain and bead dangles to the second earring make sure that you create a mirror image so that when the earrings are worn the butterflies are both on the outside ring.

Simple Wire Ring

Wire rings can be a little tricky as they are generally worked around a ring mandrel. This quick and easy design uses spiral wrapping that allows the ring base to bend in a smooth curve without special tools. You can use any small beads for the front of the ring but these little rhombus-shaped Swarovski mini beads have a wonderful sparkle.

YOU WILL NEED

40 cm (16 in) of 0.8 mm (20 awg) wire,
 gold-plated
80 cm (31½ in) of 0.6 mm (22 awg) wire,
 gold-plated
Swarovski Elements:
 Mini rhombus bead 5054, 6 mm, 2 rose
 and 1 tangerine
Jewellery tools

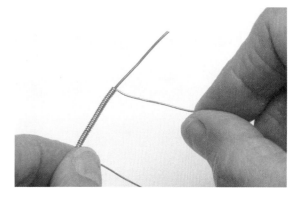

1 Arrange the thin wire at right angles to the thicker wire so that they cross in the middle of each wire. Hold one tail of the thin wire and then wrap the thicker wire with tight spirals (See Techniques, page 104).

Tip: Hold the thin wire about 10 cm (4 in) from the thick wire to get a tighter neater spiral.

2 Wrap for about 2 cm (¾ in) then change and wrap the other tail for 2 cm (¾ in) to create a closely packed spiral about 4 cm (1 9/16 in) long. The length will depend on the size of ring you want to make.

3 Form the spiral into a 'u' shape. Use snipe-nose pliers to bend one end of the thicker wire at right angles leaving a 1 mm (0.05 in) gap above the spiral. Pick up the three mini rhombus beads on this tail and wrap around the other thick wire twice just above the spiral.

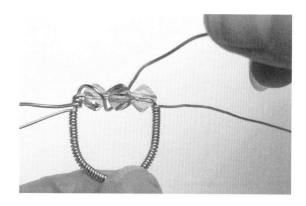

4 Check the size of the ring at this stage as you can pull the 'u' shape out a little and then wrap with the thinner wire a few more times to enlarge.

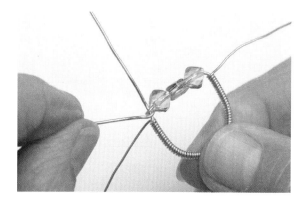

6 Wrap one of the thinner wires across the beads and then go back in the opposite direction to create an attractive crossed wrapping. Wrap the thin wire tails around at the top of the spirals and trim neatly.

5 Wind the other tail of the thicker wire around the beads a couple of times to get to the other side of the ring and then wrap the tail twice just above the spiral. Trim the two tails of thicker wire close to the ring.

Tip: When you are wrapping the beads try to keep them flat so that the rhombus shape is lying flat at the front of the ring.

Brick Stitch Ring

Bead stitching is one of the most popular beading techniques and there are lots of different patterns that can be used for making jewellery. Brick stitch is ideal for a ring as the bead fabric curves horizontally to create a tube. This design is worked with a gap in the brick stitch so that you can sew in three large round beads at the front.

YOU WILL NEED

Miyuki Delica seed beads, size 10 (2.2 mm), matte opaque orange AB (872), dura galvanized matte gold (1832F)
Swarovksi Elements:
  3 round crystal pearls 5810, 6 mm, gold
Nymo beading thread, burnt orange
Size 10 beading needle
Scissors

1 To begin the brick stitch ring, work a foundation row using matte opaque orange beads (see Techniques, pages 108–109). An average ring size is about 28 seed beads in each row. Bring the two ends together then sew back and forwards through the end beads to create a tube with the tail and working thread coming out at opposite sides.

Tip: To butt the ends together, the two rows have the same number of beads but the end bead should jut out at opposite ends on the top and bottom rows.

2 To start cylindrical brick stitch, pick up two gold seed beads and pass the needle under the thread going between the point where the working thread emerges and the next seed bead. Go back up through the last seed bead added (see Techniques, page 109–110).

3 Continue working brick stitch, picking up just one gold seed bead at a time now, taking the needle under the thread bar and back through the bead just added. Repeat to add 20 gold seed beads in total. Take the thread back through to the other side of the orange beads. Starting from step 1 again, make a second identical ring.

4 Bring the needle out on the second last gold seed bead and then work another shorter row of brick stitch, adding two beads to start as usual and then adding 19 gold beads in total. Stop with the thread coming out through the top of the end bead.

5 Line up both ring parts and begin to sew the two halves together. *Take the needle under the thread bar on the opposite half and back through the same bead where the thread emerged. Come back down through the adjacent bead. Repeat from * to finish sewing the two halves together.

6 There are seed beads on the orange band not attached to a gold bead. Bring the needle out on one of the end beads. Pick up a gold pearl and go through the same seed bead on the opposite side then come back through the adjacent seed bead and back through the pearl.

7 Sew through seed beads to come out in a middle seed bead. Add another gold pearl going back through the adjacent seed beads. Sew through seed beads to add the third gold pearl.

8 Go back through the seed beads and pearls with the needle and thread again for extra strength and then sew the thread ends in, working a half hitch knot over some of the threads between the beads before trimming.

Hair Slide

You can buy all sorts of accessories suitable for hair decorations from your local beading shop. This little hair slide has pairs of holes all along the back for threading wire and so you can use a selection of bought flower beads to decorate or make these pretty seed bead flowers following the easy instructions.

YOU WILL NEED

Seed beads, size 11 (2 mm) Toho, 90 each in turquoise (412), orange (129) and lemon (902)

6 seed beads, size 8 (3 mm), matte silver

10 m (11 yd) wire, 0.315 mm (30 awg), silver-plated

Superglue

Hair grip with mesh panel

Jewellery tools

1 Cut 6 lengths of 0.315 mm wire about 15 cm (6 in) long. To make a petal, pick up three seed beads and drop down to the middle of the wire. Take one tail and circle around to pass it back through two end seed beads.

2 Pull the tails so that the seed beads are sitting in a triangle, with a single and then two seed beads in the next row. Pick up three seed beads on one tail and pass the other tail back through the beads in the opposite direction. Pull taut to create the third row.

3 Pick up two seed beads on one tail and pass the other tail back through the beads in the opposite direction. Pull taut to complete the petal shape. Twist the wires close to the petal a couple of times to secure.

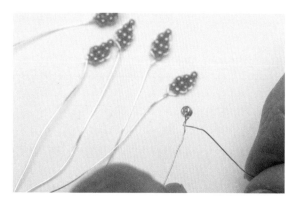

4 Make five petals in total for the flower. Trim one tail off all the petal stems. Pick up a size 8 seed bead on the last piece of wire, drop down to the middle and twist the wire once to secure.

5 Hold all the petals in a bundle and twist the wires close to the petals twice, then arrange into a flower. Thread the size 8 seed bead tails each side of the flower centre, then wrap the wire around below the flower a few times. Add a drop of superglue into the final wrapping and leave to dry.

Tip: Take care not to overwork the wire by bending it back and forwards as it will break. You can always add a new length by wrapping it around between the petals.

6 Leaving one of the size 8 seed bead tails, trim the others to create a short stub at the back of the flower. Make two flowers in each colour. Thread the wire stems one at a time into the mesh, coming back through the mesh and winding around the petals if necessary to secure. Trim the wire tails so that the cut ends are above the mesh.

Hair Band

This pretty hairband would look absolutely fabulous teemed with a pretty and feminine colourful summer dress. With so many vibrant beads it will go with just about any outfit! You can use a ready-made hairband and simply wrap it with ribbon and decorate it with beads or cover a tiara band with a rouleau tube as shown here.

YOU WILL NEED

Tiara band, silver-plated
50 cm (20 in) rouleau fabric tubing
75 cm (30 in) of 2–3 mm (1/8 in) wide satin ribbon
6 heart beads, 8 mm, coloured plastic with large holes
5 rose beads, 8 mm, plastic, bright colours
5 flower beads, 10 mm, plastic, bright colours
5 natural pearls, 2–3 mm
Sewing thread and needle
Beading thread and fine needle
Superglue

1 Feed the tiara band through the rouleau tubing. Fold the end over twice at one end to cover all the raw edges and sew in place with tiny hem stitches to secure. Stretch the rouleau then trim the fabric to leave 12 mm (½ in) beyond the tiara band. Fold over and hem this end too.

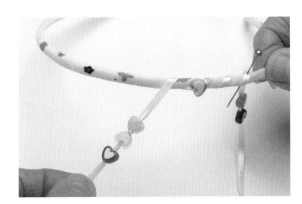

2 Pick up the heart beads on the satin ribbon, alternating the direction the beads are facing each time. Hold the middle bead on the hairband about 2 cm (¾ in) to one side of the centre. Wrap the ribbon at an angle twice over the centre of the hairband and pin the ribbon to secure.

3 Wrap the ribbon at an angle twice before positioning each heart bead in turn. Loop the ribbon around at the end of the hairband, tuck the tail under, sew to secure, then trim neatly. Repeat to finish the other side of the hairband.

4 Stick a rose bead beside each heart bead on the next diagonally wrapped ribbon. Use a drop of superglue on the satin ribbon and hold each bead in turn until the glue dries before moving to the next.

Tip: Arrange the different beads around the hairband to make sure that the colours are mixed attractively and no two adjacent beads are the same colour.

5 Secure a length of beading thread under one of the remaining diagonal ribbons. Pick up the flower bead, then a small pearl and sew back through the ribbon and rouleau fabric. Sew back and forwards under the bead to secure and then trim the thread.

6 Repeat to add the rest of the flower beads spaced out on the remaining diagonal ribbons. Add a drop of superglue under each one in turn to make sure the beads are secure.

Bag Charm

Steampunk style has brought a huge variety of different vintage charms and findings into the jewellery market and so it is easy to source unusual pieces to make this delightful bag charm. Choose the beads to match your bag so that it can hang on the outside. Alternatively, you can use the bag charm as a decorative key ring to hang in the door lock.

YOU WILL NEED

Swivel clip keyring, antique bronze
10 cm (4 in) of rollo chain, 3 mm (1/8 in) round links, antique bronze
Large key charm, antique bronze, approximately 6 cm (2½ in)
Padlock and key set charms, antique bronze
Lucite flowers: 1 large coral, and 1 small pink
Large beads, 1 oval, coral, 10–15 mm and 1 round, pink, 10 mm
2 round ceramic beads, 7 mm
3 round beads, fire-polished matt gold, 4 mm
4 round pearls, coral, 4 mm
Split ring, antique bronze, 12 mm
2 jump rings, antique bronze, 4 mm
4 decorative headpins, antique bronze
7 headpins, antique bronze
Jewellery tools

1 Use decorative headpins to make plain loop bead dangles with the large round and oval beads (see Techniques, page 105). Use plain headpins to make the ceramic beads, the pearls and the fire-polished beads into bead dangles.

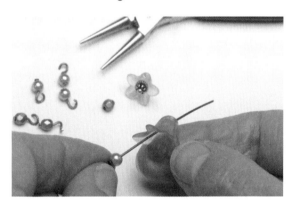

2 Make the Lucite flowers into bead dangles. Either use a decorative headpin or add a pearl for a flower centre and then add a bronze bead on the outside too before forming the loop.

3 Cut three lengths of chain approximately 1.5, 2 and 3 cm (5/8, ¾ and 1¼ in). Open the large split ring and attach to the swivel clip. Then add all three chains, in length order, onto the split ring through the end links.

4 Attach the large key charm to the middle length of chain using a jump ring (see Techniques, page 103). Attach the padlock and set of keys to the short length of chain using a jump ring.

5 Attach a large round pink bead dangle to the end of the longest chain. Add the large Lucite flower dangle to the top of the longest chain and the smaller Lucite flower halfway down.

6 Open the loop on the large oval coral bead dangle and attach to the split ring next to the shorter length of chain. Finish the dangle by attaching the smaller beads on the chains to create a balanced effect.

Felt Beaded Brooch

Felt comes in so many different colours you will be able to make a whole collection of these pretty brooches to match different clothes. As the lines are so short, the beads are simply sewn on in straight lines but can be 'couched' down by stitching over the bead string every couple of beads for extra security.

- -

YOU WILL NEED

Felt: pale green, pink, coral, peach
Seed beads: size 9 (2.5 mm), pink and
  size 11 (2 mm), lime and peach
Hex seed beads, size 11 (2 mm), gold
Beading thread, pale yellow
Beading needle, size 10
Brooch pin
Curved decoupage scissors

1 Die-cut suitable flower shapes or trace the template provided and cut patterns from paper. Pin to the felt and cut out carefully with curved scissors for accuracy. Cut two base layers, shown here in pale green.

2 Layer the smaller flowers on top of one of the pale green shapes, lining up the petals. Sew a couple of small stitches in the reverse of the felt in the middle and bring the needle up through the centre of the felt flower.

Tip: If you are using sewing thread to add the beads, use a double length for extra security.

3 Pick up a size 9 lime bead and go back down through the same hole. Come back through at the side of the bead and pick up four size 9 pink beads. Arrange the beads flat in a line out to a 'v' shape between the petals and take the needle back down at the end of the beads to the reverse side.

4 Sew five more lines of four pink
   seed beads in a star shape. *Take
   the needle through one line from the
   centre out. Pick up a size 9 lime bead
   and go back through the line of beads.
   Repeat from * to add a lime bead at
   the end of each line of pink beads.

5 Stitch a single hex bead between each
   line of pink beads near the centre.
   Add another single hex bead on each
   'v' shape on the pale pink flower.
   Bring the needle up through one of
   the doughnut beads and go back
   through the hex bead. Pick up three
   size 11 lime beads and set out in a
   straight line. Sew down through the
   felt after the beads.

6 Repeat to add lime beads all the way
   around. Add four size 11 peach beads
   on each of the coral felt petals to
   finish. Sew in the thread end on the
   reverse side.

7 Arrange the second layer of pale
   green felt at the back of the flower.
   Bring a thread out between the layers
   and then work blanket stitch all the
   way around. Sew a brooch pin just
   above centre on the reverse side.

Tip: When sewing the brooch pin on, it
   is easier to sew under the edge of the
   pin then up through the hole, working
   alternately from side to side.

Beaded Bookmark

Bookmarks are a lovely gift idea and really quick to make. Even in this electronic era it's a delight to keep your place in a diary, notebook or novel with these pretty beaded charms. The faux suede leather that connects the two clusters of beads is flat and won't damage the pages.

YOU WILL NEED

Selection of 3–4 decorative beads
4 round beads, 6 mm, in toning colours
Round bead, 8 mm, in toning colours
5 seed beads, silver, in size 11 (2 mm) and
    size 8 (3 mm)
4 ball-end headpins, silver-plated
1 m (1 yd) of 0.4 mm (26 awg) wire, silver-
    plated
2 cord crimp ends, silver-plated, 3 mm
2 jump rings, 5 mm, silver-plated
2 cm (¾ in) fine chain, silver-plated
30 cm (12 in) of 3 mm (⅛ in) wide
    Ultrasuede
Jewellery tools

1 Attach a cord crimp to each end of the ultrasuede (see Techniques, page 98). Pick up a size 8 seed bead on a ball-end headpin then add a 6 mm round bead followed by the focal bead (in this case a ceramic butterfly). Make a wrapped loop and then trim the tail. You may need to add size 11 seed beads before the wrapped loops so that the butterfly bead sits straight.

Tip: Headpins can be made from hard or soft wire. Soft wire headpins that often look bent in the packet are easier to use for wrapped loops.

2 Make a wrapped loop on one end of a 15 cm (6 in) length of 0.4mm (26 awg) wire (see Techniques, page 107). Pick up the second decorative bead for the main dangle (in this case a flower). Pre-form the next wrapped loop and attach to the butterfly headpin dangle before finishing the wrapping.

3 Cut the chain into two different lengths. Start with a 15 cm (6 in) length of 0.4 mm (26 awg) wire and pre-form a wrapped loop. Attach to the end of the longer piece of chain, finish wrapping the loop then trim the tail. Pick up a 6 mm round bead and pre-form the next loop. Add the shorter length of chain before wrapping and trimming the tail.

4 Make the last dangle with a ball end headpin, adding a size 8 seed bead to start and then an 8 mm round bead. Pre-form the loop and attach to the other end of the short length of chain before completing the wrapping. Attach both beaded pieces to one end of the Ultrasuede using a jump ring (see Techniques, page 103).

5 For the other end of the Ultrasuede, make one dangle with a size 8 seed bead and 6 mm round bead and another dangle with a size 8 seed bead, 6 mm round bead and a larger decorative bead, adding a seed bead again before wrapping the final loop.

6 Use a jump ring to attach these two wrapped loop dangles to the other cord end to finish.

Materials and Equipment

If this is your first foray into beading you will find that there are quite a few projects you can make without specialist tools or materials and you may find you have all you need in your workbox, though an inexpensive microfibre bead mat is an essential as it prevents beads from rolling onto the floor!

BEADS

Beads are the most important aspect of any design. Beading shops are wonderful places as there are so many different beads to see, from tiny seed beads to elegant strings of pearls and unusual and contemporary designs. Beads are made from all sorts of materials from plastic to semi-precious gem stones and come in a huge range of colours and finishes. It is impossible to list where to buy every bead that is used in the projects as the beads in the shops are constantly changing to reflect current trends and seasons. To create a similar design, look at the size and shape of beads and the colour balance and have fun choosing similar beads in the same colourway, or one to suit your own taste.

MATERIALS

The materials you will need are readily available in beading or craft shops or online. Just buy what you need for each project, but basic materials that you should have in your workbox include jewellery wire in 0.4, 0.6 and 0.8 mm (26, 22 and 20 awg) thicknesses and bead stringing wire – the inexpensive 7-strand wire is suitable for bracelets, and a 19-strand wire for necklaces as it is stronger and has a better drape. It is also useful to have a selection of different weights of chain.

TOOLS

It is a good idea to buy a good set of jewellery tools: snipe-nose and flat-nose pliers for general wire work, round-nose pliers for making loops and wire cutters, preferably good quality flush cutters that trim the wire end flat. Choose small, but not miniature, tools that will let you get close to the work, as jewellery is generally quite small scale. Other tools you may need are crimp pliers for securing crimp beads or tubes, and perhaps nylon-jaw pliers that can be used to straighten wire and are less likely to damage findings.

A selection of glues can be useful – jewellery glue such as E6000 or GS cement that stays flexible and so doesn't crack; epoxy resin, a very strong two-part adhesive, and gel superglue for quick-drying situations.

FINDINGS

Beads can simply be strung onto a length of cord or ribbon and tied in a knot or bow to make a basic bracelet or necklace, but for more interesting or advanced designs you need findings to create the shape, attach chain or finish off ends neatly. Look in your local beading shop or online as there is a vast array of these small, usually metal components that can be used to make jewellery and accessories much more interesting and professionally finished. Any findings you need are listed in the 'you will need' lists for the projects and you can find out how to use them in the following Techniques section.

The essentials for your workbox include jump rings that can be round or oval; use the smallest suitable jump ring size for a given situation, as it will be more secure. Headpins are one of the most useful findings – used to make bead dangles, they can be trimmed and used instead of wire to make bead links too. Choose hard wire headpins for plain loops and soft wire headpins for wrapped loops (see Techniques, pages 105–108). Fastenings come in all shapes and sizes from the basic bolt ring and lobster claw to toggle and magnetic fastenings – choose a style to suit the project so that it is secure but easy to undo and fasten.

Techniques

BASIC KNOTS
Overhand Knot

This knot has many uses in jewellery making and beading. It can be used to tie several strands together or worked as a stopper on a single cord. The double overhand knot makes a more decorative stopper.

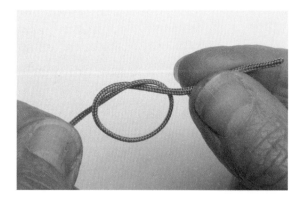

1 Circle the tail around clockwise and then take it over the main cord and bring it out in the middle of the loop. Pull both ends to firm up.

2 This variation is known as double overhand knot because you take the tail over the main cord twice before firming up.

3 Pull both ends slowly and the knot will form this figure of eight shape before tightening into a neat ball-shaped knot.

Reef Knot and Surgeon's Knot

The reef knot is used to tie two cords of equal thickness together. It can be undone by pulling one tail back toward the knot. The surgeon's knot is similar but more secure.

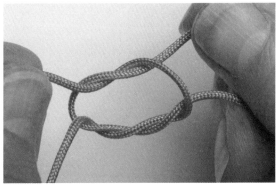

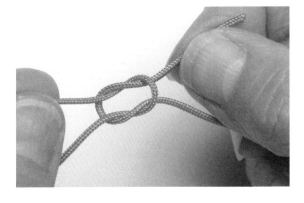

2 When tying elastic cord, use the surgeon's knot. To tie this variation, take the left cord over the right cord twice and then take the right cord over the left just the once.

1 To tie a reef knot, take the left cord over the right cord and then bring it out underneath. Then take the right cord over the left and under. Firm up by pulling on both tails.

3 Pull both tails slowly until the knot forms a neat knot. With elastic cord add a drop of glue and allow to dry before trimming the tails.

MACRAMÉ

Macramé is a versatile knotting technique that can be used in various ways to make jewellery or accessories. Although there are lots of different macramé knots, all the projects in this book use the square or flat knot. Use a macramé board or tape the cords to the work surface.

1 Secure one or two core cords the length of the finished project plus 15 cm (6 in) for finishing. Add a single working cord on each side. These working cords are four times the length of the finished project plus 15 cm (6 in) for finishing.

2 To work the first half of the square knot, take the left cord under the core cords and over the cord on the right.

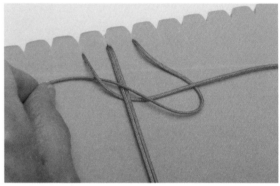

3 Then take the right cord over the core cords and pass it down through the loop formed by the left cord. Pull both working cord ends to firm up.

Tip: If you repeat this first half of the square knot again and again, you will create a round spiral braid.

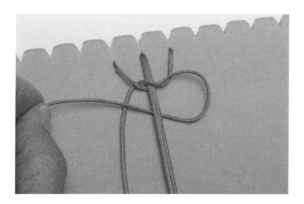

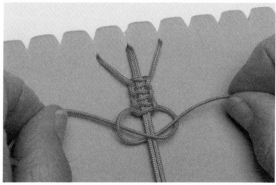

4 To work the second half of the square knot, take the right cord under the core cords and over the cord on the left.

6 Repeat from step 2 to create the braid to the length you require. If you stop, remember that the cord that is sticking up out of the knot is the one you take under the core cords next.

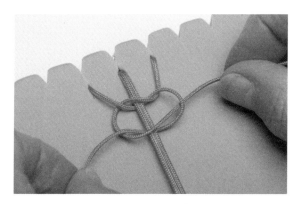

5 Then take the left cord over the core cords and pass it down through the loop formed by the right cord. Pull both working cord ends to firm up.

FINISHING ENDS

There are many different findings that can be used to cover or secure the raw ends of wire, cord or thread when making jewellery and other beaded accessories. These little metal fittings are then often used to connect a fastening of some sort – some are secured by crimping with pliers and others attached using strong glue.

Cord Ends

Choose the style of cord end to suit the type of cord or braid that you are using. Some are suitable for round cords, some for flat cords and others ideal for securing multiple cords.

2 Tiny cord ends are often made from soft metal that can be squeezed with pliers to secure the cord, wire or braid. Larger cord ends are glued in place. Put the glue into the finding rather than onto the cord.

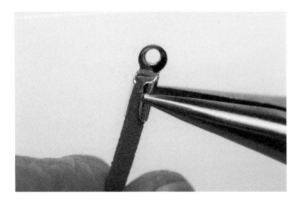

1 Cord ends with lugs can be secured with pliers. Choose a size that will fit closely around the cord. Flatten one side over the cord first and then the other side.

Ribbon Crimps

These bar-style crimps come in different lengths from about 5 mm (¼ in) to more than 2.5 cm (1 in). Initially designed to secure ribbon, they are perfect for anything from narrow Ultrasuede to macramé braids or even multiple strands.

1 Trim the end of the ribbon straight and then position inside the jaws – you can add a little jewellery glue. Use nylon-jaw pliers to close the crimp so that the metal doesn't get damaged.

2 Before securing braids such as macramé inside a ribbon crimp, stitch the strands together and then trim.

Crimps

Crimps are tiny metal findings that are either donut-shaped or tubular. They are used to secure beads or add findings to bead stringing wire (tigertail). You can either flatten the crimp or secure it more professionally with crimp pliers.

1 Crimp tubes flatten with flat or snipe-nose pliers to create a neat square. Use this technique to space beads down the wire or if the crimp is going to be hidden inside a calotte or crimp cover.

2 When working on a double wire, use crimping pliers to secure. Flatten the

crimp into an oval shape using the plain indents in the tool, shown here on the left.

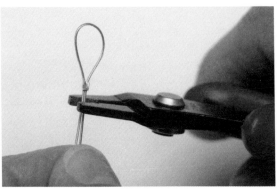

3 Move the crimp across into the next indents. Squeeze the pliers so that the dip is formed in the crimp between the two wires.

Tip: Refer to the manufacturer's recommendations so that you are using the correct crimp and tool for the wire. If a crimp shatters it is usually because it is too big.

4 Rotate the crimp and wire around 90 degrees and then use the plain indents again to squeeze the crimp so that if folds up into a neat round shape. Check that it has clamped the wire securely.

Calottes

Calottes are hinged findings that are used to cover the raw end of bead stringing wire usually in a neat professional way. Regular calottes have a hinge on the side, and clamshell calottes, which are more secure, have the hinge at the base.

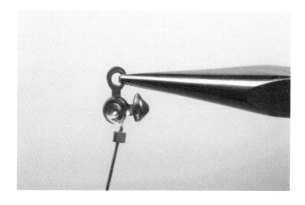

1 Flatten a crimp or secure with a crimp tool on the end of the bead stringing wire. Select a calotte that will fit over the crimp. Position the crimp so that the wire is in the slot at the base.

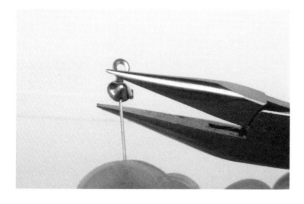

2 Close the calotte by squeezing the two sides together using flat or snipe-

nose pliers. You can further secure the calotte by squeezing the hinge itself in the pliers to flatten.

3 As clamshell calottes have a hole in the hinge, thread the bead stringing wire through the hole and then attach the crimp. You can either flatten or secure with crimp pliers.

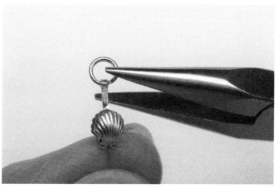

4 Close the clamshell calotte with pliers. Once you add a jump ring, fastening, or other finding to the calotte, flatten the metal loop using pliers to secure.

WIRE GUARDIANS

These small findings protect bead-stringing wire and silk thread preventing it from fraying. You can make jewellery without the guardians but it won't last as long. When working with silk thread, gimp is an alternative.

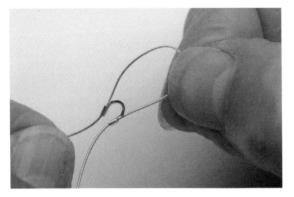

1 Choose a wire guardian that will allow the wire/thread to pass up through one side and then feed the tail over the 'u' shape and back down through the other side.

2 Feed the tail of the wire through the hole in the finding and then arrange the wire guardian so that it is sitting straight.

3 Feed a crimp over both the main wire and the tail. Push down so the crimp is close to the wire guardian and then secure the crimp with crimp pliers.

4 You can simply string beads onto the main wire and over the tail then butt up against the crimp but it is neater and more attractive to cover the crimp with a crimp cover. Use crimp pliers rather than regular pliers to close the cover over the crimp so that it keeps its neat, round shape.

JUMP RINGS

Jump rings are the most common finding used in jewellery making. To keep the round shape, don't pull the two sides apart but follow these guidelines.

1 To open, grasp both sides with the edge of flat or snipe-nosed pliers and then tilt one pair of pliers forward or back till there is a suitable gap.

3 So that there is no gap between the two ends, tilt the pliers back and forwards two or three times while applying inward pressure.

Tip: Don't use the tip of snipe-nose pliers unless working in a tight space as the jump ring can be bent out of shape.

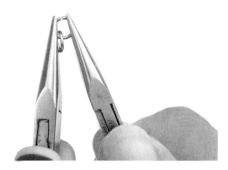

2 Pick up the second jump ring or finding and slot through the gap and then close the jump ring by reversing the tilting action.

WORKING WITH WIRE

Wire for jewellery comes in a variety of thicknesses and metals. You can buy solid metals such as sterling silver, aluminium, copper or brass, for example, or copper wires that have been plated to make silver or gold finishes, or enameled in a wide range of colours.

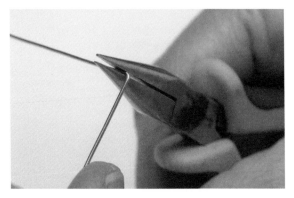

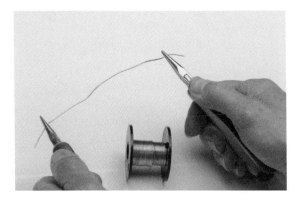

1 Before use, wire should be straightened. Pull through nylon jaw pliers or hold both ends with flat or snipe-nose pliers and pull apart firmly until straight.

2 When bending wire at a sharp angle, use flat or snipe-nose pliers to hold the wire and then fold down against the tool to create the neat bend.

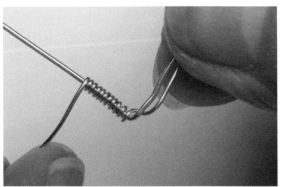

3 To wrap one wire around another, hold the thinner wire alongside the tail of the thicker wire for purchase and then wrap at right angles so that the spiralling wire is closely packed.

Plain Loops

Plain loops can be worked with hard wire headpins, eyepins or craft wire that is at least 0.6 mm (22 awg) thick and strong enough to hold the round shape in use. The thicker the wire, the larger the loop, but in general, smaller loops are stronger and less likely to pull open.

2 Hold the headpin end about 5 mm (¼ in) from the tip of the round-nose pliers so that you can just feel the cut end of the headpin on the sides of the pliers. Begin to rotate the pliers forward.

1 Pick up the beads you require on a headpin. Keeping the beads butted against the end of the headpin, bend the wire over at 90 degrees just above the beads and trim the tail to 7 mm. If you are using a thicker wire, cut the tail slightly longer.

3 Readjust the position of the pliers so that you can rotate again to bend the headpin around to form a loop. Keep easing the tail in until it touches the headpin again.

Plain loop beadlink

Beadlinks have a plain loop at each end with beads in the middle. Use craft wire that is at least 0.6 mm (22 awg) or a hardwire headpin with the flat head cut off.

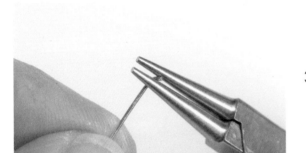

3 Insert the round-nose pliers into the loop again as shown and then bend the long tail back against the pliers to 'break the neck' and create the right angle between loop and tail.

1 Hold the end of the wire about 5 mm (¼ in) from the tip of the round-nose pliers so that you can just feel the cut end on the sides of the pliers. Begin to rotate the pliers.

4 Pick up beads and create a loop at the other end following steps for plain loop on page 105. Grasp both loops in flat- or snipe-nose pliers and tilt one pair of pliers until both loops are level.

2 Hold the wire against the pliers with your thumb and continue to reposition and rotate the pliers until the cut end of the wire touches the main wire again.

Tip: Join bead links and plain loops together or onto another finding by opening and closing in the same way as jump rings.

Wrapped Loops

Wrapped loops are more secure than plain loops and can be made with a finer wire. Use soft rather than hard wire headpins as they are easier to wrap around.

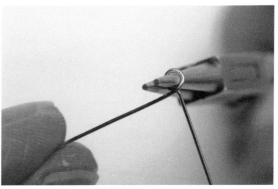

1 Bend a length of wire at right angles using flat or snipe-nose pliers so that you have a short tail sticking out to the side at least 5 cm (2 in) long.

3 Change the position of the pliers so that the jaws are horizontal and bend the tail around so that it is at right angles to the main wire. This is known as a 'pre-formed loop'

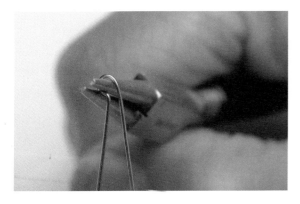

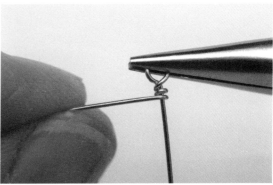

2 Change to round-nose pliers, positioning them so that the bottom jaw is tucked into the bend as shown. Bring the tail over the top of the pliers and straight down the other side.

4 Grasp the loop with flat or snipe-nose pliers and then holding the tail close to the end, wind around the main wire two or three times. Trim the tail close to the wrapping.

Wrapped Loop Bead Link

1 Once you have made the first wrapped loop add the beads onto the wire. Hold the link upright so that the beads are held close to the bottom wrapping. Grasp the wire above the beads with the tip of snipe-nose pliers. Bend over at a right angle.

2 Change to round—nose pliers and make a loop following wrapped loops on page 107. Stop before you do the wrapping at the 'pre-formed' loop stage and then attach another wrapped bead link or finding.

BRICK STITCH

Brick stitch is one of the most popular bead stitches. It can be worked as a flat fabric but as it is used to make a ring, the instructions here are for the tubular version. Use the foundation row technique as a quick way to create the first two rows of brick stitch.

Foundation Rows

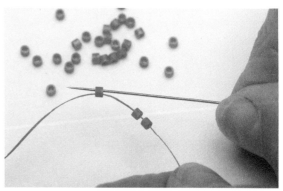

1 Pick up three seed beads and pass the needle through the first seed bead in the opposite direction (toward the end of the tail). Pull the thread taut to leave a 10 cm (4 in) tail and the three seed beads stacked together in a triangle shape.

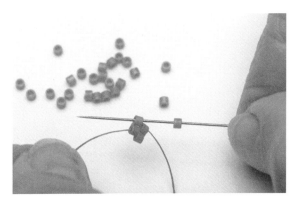

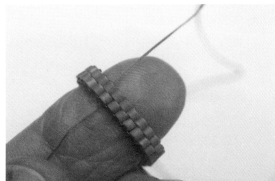

2 *Pick up a seed bead and pass the needle up through the seed bead jutting out at the end. Pick up another seed bead and pass the needle down through the seed bead jutting out at the end. Repeat from * until the band is the length required.

2 Continue to stitch in a figure of eight through the end beads two or three times to join into a tube. Finish with the tail and working thread on opposite sides.

Joining the Ends

Working Tubular Brick Stitch

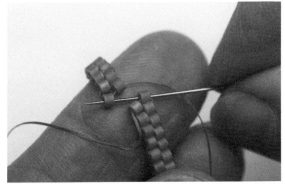

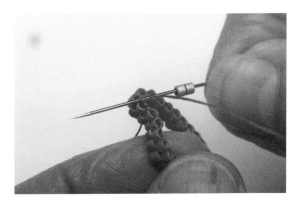

1 Stop when there is the same number of beads on each row with a bead jutting out at each end in opposite directions. Bring the ends together and sew diagonally through the two end beads.

1 Pick up two seed beads and pass the needle through under the thread bar between the bead where the thread emerges and the adjacent bead.

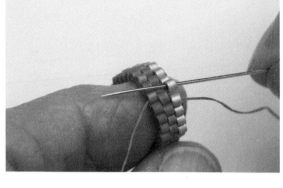

2 Pass the needle and thread back through the second bead added and pull taut so that the two beads sit side by side.

4 At the end of the round, circle the thread through the first and last beads and finish with the thread coming out of the top of the last bead added ready to start the next round at step 1 again.

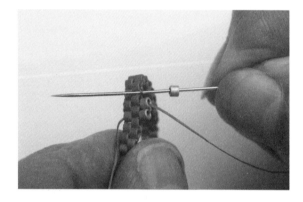

3 From now on pick up just one seed bead at a time, taking the needle under the next thread bar each time and back through the bead just added.

Template

BEADED BROOCH
Actual size.

ABOUT THE AUTHOR

Dorothy Wood is an expert beader, craft designer and author who has written more than 30 craft books on a variety of subjects and is a regular contributor to numerous craft and beading magazines. Since 2004, Dorothy has focused on beading and jewellery and in 2012 became the first UK ambassador for Swarovski Elements. Recently, she has ventured into the DVD market with her first two beginners' jewellery titles and has also started to sell kits of her jewellery designs.

www.dorothywood.co.uk
@blondorothy
blondorothy.wordpress.com
www.facebook.com/dorothywoodbeadsandcrafts

ACKNOWLEDGEMENTS
I've really loved designing the projects for this book and thoroughly enjoyed sourcing the gorgeous beads to make them. Thanks to Bead Crazy, Heavenly Beads, I-Beads and the Bead Workshop for their generosity in supplying materials. I love all aspects of creating a book from the making, to the writing and step photography and was delighted to work with the talented photographer, Ally Stuart, who took such detailed steps and delightful images of the finished projects. I'm indebted as always to the editorial team at New Holland. Thanks to Diane Ward for commissioning the book and Simona Hill for her support and editing skills. Special thanks of course go to my husband David whose generosity allows me the time to be creative.

US $19.99
UK £12.99